THE CRUCIBLE

NOTES

including
Life and Background
List of Characters
Commentaries
Critical Analysis
The Historical Background
Review Questions and Essay Topics
Appendixes
Selected Bibliography

by
Denis M. Calandra, M.A.
Department of English
University of Nebraska

and
James L. Roberts, Ph.D.
Department of English
University of Nebraska

INCORPORATED

LINCOLN, NEBRASKA   68501

CONTENTS

Life and Background

Arthur Miller was born in New York on October 17, 1915, the son of a prosperous manufacturer who lost his fortune in the crash of 1929. As a young student, Miller was apparently rather apathetic, failing several subjects and showing virtually no interest in schoolwork. After the family lost its fortune, he quit school before graduating and secured a variety of jobs, including work as a farmhand and various jobs around the New York waterfront. Through these jobs Miller learned about the life of the simple man of America who became the concern of many of his works. *A View from the Bridge* handled some aspects of waterfront work, and the movie, *The Misfits*, which incidentally starred his wife, the late Marilyn Monroe, drew from his experiences as a farmhand.

While working as a common laborer for fifteen dollars a week, Miller discovered the value of literature and began to save part of his meager salary to finance a year of college. He convinced the University of Michigan to accept him as a student even though he had never graduated from high school. At Michigan he supported himself by work on the newspaper, aid from organizations, and occasional prize money from his writings. During his college years, he began writing his first dramas; he graduated in 1938 and returned to New York, where he became associated with the theater and later with radio, writing scripts for certain shows.

Mr. Miller's concern for the common man can be seen in all his plays. His first success was *All My Sons* — a play which investigates some basic assumptions about our capitalistic society. *Death of a Salesman* can be read as a drama of the common man being defeated by a society which drains the ordinary man of his energy and then drops him. In fact, Mr. Miller's intense concern for the fate of the common man caused him to align himself with the theoretical possibilities of Communism. He was subsequently investigated by the House Un-American Activities Committee in 1947 and was cleared completely by this committee. The point, however, is that Mr. Miller, aside from being a dramatist, is also a champion for the underprivileged man.

Mr. Miller is today considered one of America's leading dramatists. Although *Death of a Salesman* is probably his most popular play — it won the Pulitzer Prize as the best play of 1949, and the movie version also won the first prize at the Venice film festival — *The Crucible* is thought by many critics to be a more unified and superior drama. It was first produced on Broadway on January 22, 1953, and ran for only 197 performances. Too many critics failed to see the value of the play because it apparently aligned itself in a limited way with the current political controversy centered upon Senator McCarthy. However, some years later the merits of the play were obvious when it ran for over 500 performances in an Off-Broadway revival. Today, with the McCarthy hearings in the past, we can evaluate the play on its own merits and come to grips with its intrinsic worth.

List of Characters

Reverend Parris

The New England minister who is mainly responsible for the belief in witches.

Betty Parris

His ten-year-old daughter, who was caught by her father dancing in the woods and pretends to see spirits.

Tituba

Reverend Parris' Negro slave who is partly responsible for teaching the children about "spirits."

Abigail Williams

Reverend Parris' seventeen-year-old niece, who leads the other children in the accusations.

Susanna Walcott

A friend of Abigail's who also joins in accusing people of being witches.

Thomas Putnam

A vindictive man with many grievances who uses the witch tales to effect his personal vengeance upon the town.

Mrs. Ann Putnam

His wife, who attributes the death of her seven infant children to supernatural causes.

Mercy Lewis

An eighteen-year-old friend of Abigail who also pretends to see witches.

Mary Warren

The girl who works for John and Elizabeth Proctor and who is also involved in accusing people of being witches.

John Proctor

A local member of the church who has opposed many of Mr. Parris' unnecessary expenditures.

Elizabeth Proctor

John's wife, who discovers that her husband has committed adultery with Abigail Williams.

Giles Corey

One of the oldest men in the community, who is brutally put to death because he challenged the proceedings of the court.

Reverend John Hale

The minister who first instigates the investigations but later sees through them and recants.

Francis Nurse

One of the most respected men of the community, who also tries to stop the investigations.

Rebecca Nurse

A lady of immense goodness and respect who is later accused of being a witch.

Ezekiel Cheever

One of the men appointed by the court to help in the arrest of the supposed witches.

Marshal Herrick

The man who is in charge of arresting all of the accused witches.

Judge Hathorne

One of the judges sent to examine the people accused of being witches.

Deputy Governor Danforth

A special judge sent for this occasion, who is dedicated to removing all witches and who will not allow anyone to tamper with his authority.

Sarah Good

A pathetic old beggar woman who is one of the first to be accused of being a witch.

Hopkins

The jailer.

Commentaries

NOTE: The division of the scenes was supplied and is generally determined by the entrance or exit of a major character or group of characters. This division is made to aid the reader in following the commentaries.

ACT I

(Scene 1)

Scene 1 comprises the opening action and ends with Reverend Parris' going downstairs to lead the congregation in a psalm. The imagery in the opening stage directions gives the general impression of bleakness and restriction. The room's air of clean spareness is in one sense the stock image of the perfect Puritan household. Everything is harsh, spare, and constricted. But more important are the physical manifestations of a situation like the one in Salem. The very elementary problem of survival against a hostile wilderness dictated to the Puritans the need for a strongly unified government. Their theocracy, which united them "from top to bottom by a commonly held ideology whose perpetration was the reason and justification for all their sufferings," provided a form of close unity. As the "hostility" of the wilderness became less and less of a problem the need for strict government control decreased. As the society became more and more secure, greater and greater individual freedoms became possible, and this greater individual freedom clashed with the already existing theocracy. A panic resulted on the side of the already designated authority which was struggling to retain its control over the individual.

Another partial explanation suggested for the witch-hunts is the fact that they gave everyone in the strict Puritan society an opportunity to confess his sins in public. Still another motive for condemning one's neighbors was the general greed and jealousy over land ownership which had developed in the small community. The battle over land and old grievances "could be settled on a plane of heavenly combat between Lucifer and the Lord."

Parris is first presented as an almost pitiful man. He seems like a frightened, trapped animal, terribly worried about the stability of his position in the town. When we see that he is actually more concerned about his position than about his ailing daughter he loses our pity, however. Even when he questions Abigail about what went on in the woods he is more interested in covering himself before his "enemies find out" than acting as the true minister and looking after the moral welfare of his flock.

Directly as the play opens, we feel the tremor of "witchcraft" in the air. At first Parris does not want to acknowledge this, however, because it would reflect upon him; but soon he is forced to become involved.

ACT I

(Scene 2)

Left alone with Betty Parris and some other girls, Abigail Williams (Parris' niece) threatens the others if they reveal the truth about their dancing in the forest.

This scene presents the girls who will accuse dozens of people of witchcraft. The fact that the girls are trying to conceive of some way in which to escape punishment for having been caught dancing in the woods is clearly revealed to us. The horror of the situation is in our awareness that the girls will make irresponsible accusations and cause the deaths of twenty people by doing so.

Later, in a crucial point in the play, Mary Warren will falter under pressure from Abigail Williams. In this scene we are prepared for her later weakness as we see her intimidated by the stronger willed Abigail.

If witchery, *per se,* does not exist, at least the occult practices of Abigail (drinking a blood charm to kill Goody Proctor, for instance) and of the other girls seem enough to lead one to suspect witchcraft. Abigail *is* evil. There is something dangerous about her. The fact that she acquires so much power later in the play reflects that the society has some inherent weakness in it.

Early in the scene, Miller does provide a realistic motivation for the accusations of witchcraft. Parris actually saw his daughter, his niece, and the Negro slave dancing in the forest and participating in questionable activities. Their activity is diametrically opposed to all Puritan codes of ethics. (See section on Puritan Concepts of the Devil and Witches.) Parris contributes to the later accusations by planting the seeds in the minds of the young girls. He tells them that "Abominations are done in the forest—" and later wonders if they drank blood or used frogs in their ceremonies—all are things connected through superstition with the general idea of witchcraft.

Central to the entire play is the conflict between Goody (Elizabeth) Proctor and Abigail Williams. Even though they never face each other on the stage, the relationship between the Proctors and Abigail is central to the progress of the dramatic action. We hear, then, the first mention of this conflict when Abigail tries to explain her dismissal from the Proctor household. Later, Abigail's resentment will lead her to accuse Goody Proctor of being a witch.

As an introduction to the character of Thomas Putnam, Miller explains some of the motivations behind Putnam's involvement in the witch-hunt. Putnam is vindictive in shouting "Witch" at some of the more responsible members of the community because his wife's brother-in-law had formerly been rejected by them as Salem minister. Onstage, of course, none of these motives are revealed in the dramatic action. Consequently, in reading the play, we have a fuller understanding of the characters than would an audience viewing the dramatic presentation.

ACT I
(Scene 3)

John Proctor, a respected farmer, arrives to retrieve his servant Mary Warren, and as soon as he is left alone with Abigail Williams, she reminds John Proctor of how they loved each other before John's wife dismissed her. John denies his love and while they are arguing, Betty sits up in bed and begins screaming.

Miller mentions in an introductory character sketch that Proctor has "come to regard himself as a kind of fraud." A central theme of the play concerns Proctor's attempts to come to terms with himself within his own society. "What is John Proctor, what is John Proctor?" he will shout in the last act.

Abigail is a type of Dionysian element in the play. She is the embodiment of raw sexuality, who, at one point, becomes the tempter of John Proctor. Basically, she lusts after him. This lust will motivate her to accuse John Proctor's wife of being a witch so that she will be able to have John for herself. Yet, in this scene she denies that there is any such thing as witchcraft, and tells Proctor that her activity in the woods was nothing more than dancing. This sets up the conflict in John Proctor because he knows that all the accusations are false. But to reveal his knowledge will require that he admit that he is a lecher.

ACT I
(Scene 4)

Parris quickly returns as soon as he hears his daughter's cries. He and Proctor argue about the obligations of the community to its minister. The scene concludes with Proctor and Corey's argument about the rights to some land and lumber.

Rebecca Nurse, who "exudes gentleness" and who is respected by all, is later to be cried out for a witch. She is so far from anything like a witch that later on when she is accused and hanged as one, we can only reflect on the absolute absurdity of the proceedings. Rebecca Nurse is a symbol of real Order and Wisdom who, when she first senses strife between Parris and Proctor, tries to arbitrate the difficulties; she is aware of grumblings in the society and sues for peace. Her ultimate execution is indicative of the chaos which the demon-hunters inflict upon the entire community.

We also realize that the issue at hand is not merely witchery, but that it is a combination of strife over matters of politics, land ownership, power struggles, and personal vengeance. Proctor and Parris argue matters of church politics and policies; the Putnams and the Nurses are contesting each others' rights to certain plots of land; Putnam is out for personal vengeance because his candidate was not selected as minister, and later on, on a larger scale, the judges, as representative power symbols in the total community, struggle against individuals to retain their vested power. Giles Corey is seen as a contentious old man.

Parris argues that the individual man must obey the church or the church will collapse. Proctor differs because he believes in the right of every man to speak his own mind. Proctor is set up as the individual who is revolting from the restrictions of too much authority. He does not like "the smell of this authority."

ACT I
(Scene 5)

The Reverend Hale, an authority on witches, arrives, and John Proctor, who knows that the girls are pretending, leaves in disgust. After questioning the girls and hearing various stories, Reverend Hale is suspicious. He sends for the Negro slave Tituba, who, being threatened with her life, confesses that she has consorted with the Devil. The other girls also begin to name people who have bewitched them.

Hale is a somewhat admirable but problematical character whose very "noble" ideals happen to be far enough short of the truth to produce tragic results. He views himself as a veritable right-hand man of the Lord, purging the community of Lucifer. He is a learned and knowledgeable man, but he does set into action forces which bring about an evil destructive state of chaos.

In the interlude, Miller explains the type of McCarthyism (see section on McCarthyism) which is present in any period of history: one always automatically assigns to one's enemies an eternal alliance with the Devil. In Salem, the enemy is at least partially represented by Proctor, who is acting as an individual and thus breaking away from the established authority. As such, he is a threat to the community, and consequently will be considered as being aligned with the Devil.

As a respected figure in his specialized field—witchcraft— Reverend Hale is a type who will be well respected in the community. Unfortunately, later in the drama when Hale recants his views, he will no longer be respected because the witch-hunt will already have gone too far. Notice how much Hale emphasizes in his first speeches that the books he carries are weighted with "authority." The conflict between the individual freedom of the human being and the established authority that demands obedience is thus further emphasized.

One of Hale's early statements is "We cannot look to superstition in this. The Devil is precise." This line, according to Miller's own testimony, never raised a laugh in an audience, yet it is basically absurd. As is later pointed out, however, the honest belief was that the Devil is so subtle that man cannot discern his invisible devices.

Hale's interrogation of Tituba shows him confusing her by his rhetoric and rapid-fire questions, and extracting from her exactly the information he desires to hear, whether it actually be true or not. He asks her whether there was a mouse or a frog in the kettle; he knows all the particulars about witchcraft and more or less plants the answers that he seeks.

Rebecca Nurse is seen to have a certain amount of antipathy to the entire proceeding. She departs firm in the belief that the charge of witchcraft is totally absurd. By leaving to pray to God, she insinuates that the proceedings themselves are more closely associated with the Devil.

GENERAL COMMENTARY ON ACT I

Ultimately, the central figure of the drama must be seen to be John Proctor. His function in the first act is not entirely clear, but it is significant to distinguish his purpose in each individual act. Basically, Miller is working with the theme of how much the individual citizen must be committed to the society in which he lives. In an earlier play, *All My Sons*, Miller had shown how man must become a part of all humanity, must be committed to the complete society of mankind. In this early play, he had rejected the type of person who places his individual self or family above that of all mankind. Essentially, Proctor's main problem will be how much is he willing to make a commitment to society. In the first act, he tries to avoid any responsibility for the witch-hunt and simply leaves, washing his hands of the entire episode. Miller will rapidly let the reader know that no man can simply dismiss a crucial crisis in his society and that no man can live his own private life, ignoring the events transpiring around him. The community's problems are crises which concern each and every human being, and if a man tries to avoid involvement, he is leaving himself open to serious charges.

John Proctor, thus, tries to ignore the absurd charges of witchcraft and attempts to retire to the privacy of his own home. In the next act, however, we will see that he will be drawn more directly into the events because his own wife will be charged with being a witch. With this accusation, John Proctor can no longer pretend to be uninvolved, and must take some action. (Further development of this theme will be found in the General Commentary on Act II.)

ACT II
(Scene 1)

Some days later, John Proctor discovers that his servant Mary Warren is going to the court, against his commands. Furthermore, the court has promised to hang many people if they do not confess. Elizabeth Proctor wants John to go to the court and expose Abigail Williams as a fraud, but John is hesitant because of his past relationship with Abigail.

The scene at the opening of Act II is in striking contrast to the frenzied conclusion to Act I. John Proctor's home (his wife in the kitchen singing to the children, etc.) is a symbol of the domestic tranquility upon which the unity and strength of Salem depends. This is obviously meant to be contrasted with the furious lunacy connected with the witch-hunt, and to the nervous fear which pervades Parris' home. The trials, as attempts to secure unity and peace in the community, were total failures. One concrete embodiment of this in the play is the utter havoc which is wrought in the once peaceful Proctor household.

This is the first instance of Elizabeth prodding her husband to do his duty. She tells him he must go to Salem and try to stop the hideous witch trials. Furthermore, the first instance of disorder is seen in that there is a minor insurrection in the Proctor house as Mary Warren refuses to obey orders from her master and insists upon going into Salem.

In many traditional dramas, the central character is often confronted during the play with a mistake that he committed in the distant past. The importance of this past mistake is often in the fact that it prevents the main character from acting freely in the present situation. Thus, as King Lear committed an act of folly in rejecting Cordelia, and must suffer for his mistake, John Proctor is seen to be forced into a situation where he cannot act freely and must suffer for his past mistake in having an affair with Abigail. The drama hinges upon the fact that Proctor is personally involved with one of the accusers and cannot face his dilemma entirely openly.

The relationship with Abigail emphasizes another central motif in the play. Throughout the play Proctor must come to grips with himself by accepting certain aspects of his character and by learning "who he is." He says to Elizabeth when she is making insinuations: "Let you look sometimes for the goodness in me, and judge me not." He tells her, then, not to judge him, and this is important because Proctor must come to the realization that he has to judge himself and must make a commitment. In this scene, his wife is making a judgment for him; he is still trying to evade his responsibility.

ACT II
(Scene 2)

Mary Warren returns from the court and reveals that Elizabeth Proctor's name had been mentioned as a possible witch. Elizabeth warns John that Abigail Williams wants her dead so that she can marry him.

In the broadest terms, Proctor is now forced into more involvement than he had previously desired. He does not voluntarily choose to go to Salem and denounce the proceedings and Abigail, but is coerced into the decision by his wife. He is being pushed into a position which he does not want to assume, thus, the commitment is not voluntarily his. It will only be in later acts that he will realize the need for personal commitment.

Our first information about the court proceedings—from Mary Warren—tells us of the flimsy evidence upon which the people are being convicted. For example, some time ago when Goody Osborne ("Osburn") came begging, Mary Warren took sick immediately afterward. This is supposed to be proof that Goody Osborne is a witch. The logical fallacy is obvious — "*post hoc, ergo propter hoc.*" On such shoddy evidence, Goody Osborne is convicted as a witch and is to be hanged.

Goody Proctor will later be accused as a witch because a poppet (rag doll) will be found in her house. In this scene we see that Mary Warren herself brought the rag doll into the house and gave it to Elizabeth Proctor.

ACT II
(Scene 3)

Reverend Hale appears and questions the Proctors about their religious views. Elizabeth cannot believe in witches if she has herself been accused of being one.

The first people to be implicated as witches were not respectable people in the community, but now as the fever of the witchcraft trials grows in intensity, more and more respectable members of the community are being implicated. The absurdity of the entire proceeding comes more and more to light as such people as Goody Proctor and Goody Nurse are "somewhat mentioned." This seems to be the method of this type of "witch-hunt," whether it be in the Salem trials of 1692 or an American reactionary pursuit of Communist demons. People are first "somewhat mentioned," then slandered or condemned.

Parris is associated with Mammon throughout the play. In the first part, he grumbles that he is underpaid. Now Proctor criticizes the golden candlesticks and the desire of the minister to own material things. Proctor "the individual" has taken it upon himself to be openly critical of a representative of "authority": Parris. Proctor sees a flaw in the character of the minister in his inordinate desire for material goods.

As a Puritan, Proctor must attend church on the Sabbath, yet he despises the minister. The individual is thus caught up between his personal beliefs and his pledged allegiance to the state, which in Salem was synonymous with the church. He is, in fact, in error when he refuses to attend church and refuses to have his children baptized. Proctor rejects Hale's statement that since Parris is ordained "the light of God is in him." At this point, Proctor is possibly functioning as the absolute individual who creates his own private world apart from the larger realm of society. Miller's condemnation of this aspect of Proctor's character is interestingly akin to Plato's dictum that man does not correct a bad law by submitting to it. Proctor cannot correct the bad situation existing in the church by avoiding church attendance or by avoiding contact with Parris. Ultimately, he must make a real commitment to a world larger than his own.

ACT II
(Scene 4)

The constable arrives at the Proctors' house with a warrant for Elizabeth's arrest. She is accused of having "poppets" in the house with which she bewitched Abigail Williams. The only poppet in the house is the one which Mary Warren owns. After Elizabeth leaves with the constable, John Proctor tries to make Mary Warren go to the court to declare that Abigail is a liar, but she warns him that Abigail will accuse him of lechery if he interferes.

As soon as Reverend Hale hears that Rebecca Nurse has been accused, he says "if Rebecca Nurse be tainted, then nothing's left to stop the whole green world from burning." In a sense this is prophetic because the entire world of Salem *will* soon become tainted. Yet, Reverend Hale has difficulty in denying the charges. As a minister and as an expert on the "Black Arts," he reminds everyone that "until an hour before the Devil fell, God thought him beautiful in Heaven." His personal feelings tell him that a person like Rebecca Nurse could not be a witch, but all of his training has taught him that Rebecca could be possessed by the Devil. His Puritan doctrine has also taught him that the Devil is attacking everywhere and everyone and he can therefore readily accept the fact that many seemingly innocent people have been deceived by the powers of the Devil.

In contrast to people like Proctor who do not wish to become involved in society, we have the characters of Herrick and Cheever, who escape involvement by maintaining that they are the passive instruments of the state. Cheever and Herrick refuse to take responsibility for their acts by saying "the law binds me . . . I cannot budge." The point Miller makes is that the law should not bind a person if the law is corrupt. Man does not correct a bad law by yielding to it. This is what happened so often in Nazi Germany in the 1930's; too many people used the excuse that they were only following orders.

Abigail's fanaticism is seen in the fact that she rams a needle into her own stomach in order to implicate Elizabeth Proctor. The use of the poppet as a means of implicating Goody Proctor depicts one of the most primitive beliefs connected with witchcraft: that is, a person could put a hex on another person by making an image and torturing that image.

Proctor immediately sees that the real issue is "vengeance walking in Salem." This knowledge, reinforced by his wife's arrest, will force him to become more and more involved. In his anger over his wife's arrest, he accuses Hale of being a "Pontius Pilate" and later on tells him that he is a coward: "though you be ordained in God's own tears, you are a coward now!" What Proctor fails to see is that he too has been acting as a Pontius Pilate and as a coward because he has been attempting to escape any type of involvement. Even further, Proctor still refuses to go into the court and accuse Abigail openly, but instead tries to coerce Mary Warren into going into the court. When reminded that Abigail will accuse him of lechery, however, he realizes how degenerate Abigail is, and finally resolves to go with Mary Warren to the court.

GENERAL COMMENTARY ON ACT II

Act II opens with a tranquil and domestic scene in Proctor's house. As a series of crises develops, the dramatic intensity grows until the act closes with John Proctor crying out in anguish over the fate which has befallen his wife. The individual, secluded in his quiet household, cannot totally escape the frenzy which is transpiring in the town.

In Act I, Proctor had attempted to wash his hands of the entire witch-hunt and retire to the private world of his farm. He rapidly discovered that man cannot escape from the activities of his society: at first Proctor hears that his servant is an official of the court and that his wife has been "somewhat mentioned" as a witch by the woman with whom he had fornicated. Finally, the turmoil of the town intrudes upon John's isolation as Cheever comes to arrest Goody Proctor for a witch.

During the course of the act, we still observe John Proctor attempting in any way possible to avoid direct involvement. It is only after his wife is arrested that he is forced to acknowledge some type of commitment to his society. Because of his previous sin with Abigail, he knows the debased morality of this accuser, but to become involved would be to destroy his own name. As he hesitates, his wife is placed under arrest on the flimsy excuse that she keeps poppets in the house. Furthermore, John knows that Abigail, who had worked in the Proctor house, is aware that there are no poppets in the house except the one which Mary Warren carried home. Reacting to this inconsequential evidence, Proctor knows that it is not always the accuser who is holy, and he resolves to take some step toward commitment.

ACT III
(Scene 1)

At the court, Proctor brings Mary Warren to testify and is accused of trying to undermine the court. When he joins forces with two other respected people and presents a petition with ninety-one signatures, the judges order each of the people summoned to determine who is against the court.

The scene takes place in the Salem meetinghouse, which is described in terms suggesting heaviness and a forbidding atmosphere. When Danforth appears, we see that he measures his power by the number of people whom he has condemned to death — over four hundred people. Danforth is a grave man who will allow nothing to interfere with his zeal in his position. Hathorne is described as "a bitter, remorseless Salem judge." All of the functionaries are totally conscious of their power and authority, which is being questioned by Proctor and the other men who criticize the proceedings.

The judges' failure to allow any type of opposition suggests a weakness in the power structure of the community. As soon as someone offers some evidence which questions the court's authority, that person is immediately suspected of being a witch. With this paradoxical situation, the people become increasingly reluctant to criticize the court, and they allow it to go to greater extremes.

Danforth, however, is the symbol of real authority, in significant contrast to Parris, who seems closer to a lunatic fringe. As soon as someone comes to the court, Parris screams hysterically that an attempt is being made to overthrow the court.

This act shows a significant change in Proctor's character. Previously, he had worked only for his own individual ends, and desired only to live an uninvolved life. He is again offered this opportunity when Danforth asks him if he will be satisfied now that Goody Proctor has received a year's reprieve. But Proctor cannot accept this compromise. He now sees that he must act for his friends also.

The statement that Danforth makes about the court smacks of the McCarthy hearings of the early 1950's. Danforth's statement that "a person is either with this court or he must be counted against it, there be no road between" echoes almost verbatim McCarthy's often-flung accusation that those who opposed his hearings were Communists. In a sense, Miller agrees with both Danforth and McCarthy, although, of course, his ideology is opposed to theirs. The point Miller wants to impress us with is that no matter what a man's beliefs happen to be he must be prepared to assert himself in defending them. In this play he could not accept the type of men who would merely sit back and watch such travesties of justice take place.

ACT III
(Scene 2)

John Proctor gets Mary Warren to testify that the other girls are frauds and only pretending. Reverend Hale wants Proctor to get a lawyer, but the judges want to question the girl immediately.

The actual motive of greed for property as a cause for the witch trials is now revealed. Giles Corey accuses Thomas Putnam: "This man is killing his neighbors for their land!" Also, the strength of the community can only exist if all the people are united under one bond, represented by the symbols of authority. But, paradoxically enough, and contradicting their own purpose, the authority symbols as we see them in Salem court can only keep "unity" by holding the people under a yoke of fear. Even Reverend Hale recognizes this when he tries to defend the unknown accuser: "We cannot blink it more. There is a prodigious fear of this court in the country—"

To reaffirm the court's authority Danforth maintains that "no uncorrupted man may fear this court" and then turns to the innocent Giles Corey and places him under arrest "in contempt of this court." Since these sentences follow one another, the absurdity of the court's logic proves to be pathetically humorous.

Hale had previously been certain of his position and confident in the proceedings of the court, but now he is altering his views. He begins to doubt the court, making several efforts to obviate some of its authoritative demands. In this scene we have the first intimation of a change in Hale which will finally lead him to reverse his position entirely.

Hale wants a lawyer to present Proctor's case, but Danforth refuses to have lawyers because they would only call up extraneous witnesses. In the case of witchcraft, he explains, only the demon and the victim are important, and since the demon is invisible one can only look to the words of the victim. Witches are part of the invisible world and commit invisible crimes; thus the testimony of the children is the only thing of relevance. Actually, Danforth is saying that he and the court alone will determine the efficacy of the evidence; he is also denying the due process of the law.

ACT III
(Scene 3)

The judge sends for the other girls, and as Abigail Williams denies the charges, Proctor accuses her of being a whore. The judge sends for Elizabeth to corroborate this testimony, but Elizabeth tries not to implicate her husband in the crime of lechery and does not support John's accusation. Suddenly, Mary Warren gives way under pressure from Abigail and accuses Proctor of witchcraft.

Both the authority and the absurdity of the court are evident in Danforth's instructions to Mary Warren. He tells her that she is bound to go to prison for lying now or for having lied in the past, thus leaving her little chance to tell the truth. This is the same type of general instruction we find when the judge tells the accused that if they do not confess they will hang for being witches. The court hearings are a combination of fustian on Danforth's part, outright lying on the parts of Abigail and Parris, and a general suppression of all those with an honest claim. The climax, of course, is the hysteria precipitated by the girls' crying out and the almost comical awe which all of this instills in the previously severe judge of men — Danforth.

In a sense Elizabeth is acting directly against her nature when she lies to save her husband's good name — the result is tragic. By lying she condemns all involved; yet, she is the one who will in the last act induce Proctor to be honest with himself. However, in another sense she doesn't lie. The question is worded "Is your husband a lecher!" Taken in the present tense, she honestly answers that he is not. Had the question been placed in the past tense—"Was your husband a lecher" or "Has your husband ever committed lechery," she might have answered otherwise.

After the court has accepted the evidence of the "possessed" children, Proctor denounces the court, claiming that "God is dead," and by so doing virtually damning himself to hell. But in terms of the transpiring events, Proctor means that if such things as these outrageous trials are allowed to continue then God must be absent or "dead."

By the end of this act, Hale has come to a complete reversal of his earlier position. Now he is the man of reason who, seeing that the children are irresponsible fanatics, denounces the court and leaves.

GENERAL COMMENTARY ON ACT III

As long as possible, Proctor avoids becoming directly involved in Salem's affairs. Rather than make a personal commitment, he first tries to evade issues by legal devices. He attempts to use Mary Warren's deposition to illustrate to the court the error it is committing. He does everything possible before accusing Abigail of adultery, thus implicating himself.

John becomes more committed to society when he refuses to take Danforth's offer to accept his wife's reprieve and leave the court to its business. Proctor refuses because the wives of too many of his friends are also accused of being witches.

Only after Mary falters in her testimony does John Proctor realize that he must become fully committed. He then accuses Abigail of being a whore and, as a result of this accusation, he is himself accused of being a witch. Thus, his commitment leads to his imprisonment. This concept is seen not only through Proctor but also through the character of Giles Corey. Giles tries to bring evidence before the court and is ultimately arrested.

ACT IV
(Scene 1)

Tituba and another woman, Sarah Good, are in jail discussing the appearance of the Devil.

Time has progressed in the play—as in the actual trial of 1692—from spring, a season of rebirth and life, to fall, the season traditionally associated with decay and imminent death. Initially, we recognize a flavor of comic relief in this first scene. Two loony hags who think they are really witches are depicted discussing the Devil and his attributes in various parts of the world. But the scene also functions as something more than just comic relief; symbolically represented are the arrival of real chaos and the disintegration of order in the community. Homeless orphans are wandering the streets; livestock are aimlessly roaming the countryside; farms have fallen into waste. When Sarah says that the Devil is coming, she is not indeed far from wrong.

ACT IV
(Scene 2)

Reverend Hale arrives and tries to get John Proctor and others to confess to being witches so that they will not be hanged.

The use of the word "authority" grows in importance during these scenes. Danforth complains that Parris has usurped authority by coming to talk to the prisoners on his own, and by allowing Hale to do likewise. The entire situation presents Danforth with a troublesome dilemma. There is danger of riot and rebellion if he carries out the court order to hang Rebecca Nurse and the others, but weakness here would be tantamount to relinquishing his power. "There will be no postponement" is his final decision.

The mistake Danforth and the other judges make is in equating the "law" with absolute right. They cannot understand the concept that to be just the law must also often be supple. As an authoritative figure Danforth can see nothing but the pure letter of the law. His refusal to acknowledge any type of rebellion in the neighboring town is typical; his words are explicit: "I should hang ten thousand that dared to rise against the law, and an ocean of salt tears could not melt the resolution of the statutes."

Only because there is immediate danger for himself does Parris sue for the lives of Proctor and the others. As he frets about the prison trying to get the prisoners to confess, the image of Parris as a petty, frightened animal magnifies. His own dilemma is similar to Danforth's, but note their contrasting motives — Danforth, though in error, is concerned with the "sacredness" of the law; Parris is selfishly scrambling for his position in Salem and for his life.

The fact that Abigail has stolen the thirty-one pounds (about $1,550 in modern terms) indicates that her testimony should be questioned, but Danforth and Parris refuse to do so. The absurdity of the entire proceedings is apparent in Danforth's statement "I cannot pardon these when twelve are already hanged for the same crime. It is not just." At this point we wonder about the justice of hanging more innocent people simple to justify earlier hangings.

The reappearance of Hale on the scene presents a practical difficulty for Proctor because the minister offers an apparently logical solution to the problem which is not, we think, what Proctor considers the "honorable" solution. Reasonable as well as expedient, Hale's argument magnifies the difficulty of Proctor's choice: "life is God's most precious gift; no principle, however glorious, may justify the taking of it. . . . God damns a liar less than he that throws his life away for pride." This seems to be the rationale that a modern realist would accept and also the rationale that Proctor would like to accept.

ACT IV
(Scene 3)

Elizabeth and John discuss whether or not he will confess to being a witch. He does not want to die such a useless death and plans to make the false confession.

Proctor wants to confess, but he tries to shirk his own responsibility by asking Elizabeth what to do. He also seems to be begging her to condone his own course of action—his own desire to escape the gibbet. He is not yet able to stand alone in his convictions.

The only reason that Proctor has refused to sign the confession is that he refuses to give such dogs as the judges the satisfaction of having a good man sign over to their side. But subsequently, it later becomes a matter of honor when he sees his friends suffering. He then accepts the honor of his friends and becomes committed to his fellow men. He finally stands firmly in the face of adversity for the sake of his own values and not just for spite.

ACT IV
(Scene 4)

John Proctor makes the confession, but when he discovers that it is to be made public and hung upon the church door, he retracts because this would also condemn his friends as witches. He chooses to die and preserve his good name.

In this scene, John Proctor attempts to preserve his own life; he cannot see himself as a saint. He asks himself: "God in

Heaven, what is John Proctor, what is John Proctor." This is the key to his personality because throughout the play, he has been trying to answer this question. At first he succumbs and signs the confession in order to save his life. But shortly afterward, faced with the possibility of condemning his friends, he recants, takes his confession, and throws it into the face of his accusers. "I speak my own sins; I cannot judge another. I have no tongue for it." By doing so he partially answers the question of "What is John Proctor" by asserting his own view of himself. John Proctor cannot live with the lie, so he will die by his own honesty.

Critical Analysis

GENERAL MEANING: AN INTERPRETATION

A study of Arthur Miller's *Crucible* as dramatic literature can be approached from several directions. Once we realize that the topical allusions to the McCarthy hearings of the early 1950's are relevant to the drama only insofar as they bear a similarity to the kind of outrage committed in Salem in 1692 – and indeed to proceedings of equal injustice in any age – thus adding strength to the author's larger thematic concerns and effectively bringing the problem "into our own backyard," so to speak, we can then readily dismiss a scrutiny of the play from the "McCarthy angle" as being of mostly historical interest.

Totally integrated, and depending upon one another for effect, there remain two areas of conflict within the play. Of primary significance is the crisis which arises when, as Miller himself put it, there is a "conflict between a man's raw deeds and his conception of himself." The struggle within John Proctor to achieve an honorable conception of himself and to fit his "raw deeds" into a pattern established by that conception comprises the single most important element in the play. Of general thematic consequence is the framework within which this individual tragedy takes place, a framework which sets in opposition those symbols of authority who fear the dwindling of their control in society on the one hand, and the forces of individualism on the other, which insistently assert themselves despite the iron-firm grip of theocracy.

To proceed from the larger thematic framework of the play to the individual tragedy of John Proctor, attempting always to indicate how the two are integrated, is one logical approach to an interpretation of the play.

The untamed wilderness and generally adverse conditions which the early Puritans faced in the New World necessitated the establishment of a strongly unified community. It was a simple choice between strict discipline and annihilation — the failure of the earlier Jamestown settlement, a community without a strong disciplinary government, only added strength to the logic of the Puritans' position. By 1692 the struggle for survival was not as immediate a problem as it was in the first few decades of the seventeenth century, but although the historical situation had altered considerably, the identical theocratic government of the first Puritans, replete with severe discipline and strictures in every area of individual life, survived. The confrontation between the established authoritarian hierarchy and those individuals seeking self-expression was inevitable. In *The Crucible* this clash takes the form of John Proctor, and to a lesser degree John Hale, against the Salem officials at first, and then against the entire order of Puritan society as represented by Danforth and Hathorne.

To express it in more universal terms, the problem with which both the symbols of authority and the new individualists are concerned, whether they realize it as such or not, is the traditional breakdown of Order, and the consequent onslaught of Chaos. What differentiates them, and provides the meat for most of the dramatic conflict within the play, is their widely divergent opinions of exactly what is causing this Chaos. Parris, the Salem minister and Proctor's immediate superior, exclaims that "There is either obedience or the church will burn like Hell is burning." The church in theocratic Salem is identical with the state and the community and will surely crumble if unquestioning obedience falters in the least.

The fact that this obedience *is* to be unquestioning becomes an awesome reality when the witch trials begin: life and death hang in the balance between obedience and dissension. "But you must understand, sir," explains Danforth, "that a person is either with this court or he must be counted against it, there be no road between." And being "counted against" the court in most cases is tantamount to being a candidate for hanging. Proctor, on the other hand, "has come to regard himself as a kind of fraud" as long as he remains obedient to an authority which he cannot respect. Parris' "hell and damnation" style of preaching and his preoccupation with material values—an example of which is his insistence that the community provide golden candlesticks for his pulpit—lead Proctor to the realization that here is no authority demanding respect, but rather something with the pungent odor of corruption to it. "I like not the smell of this 'authority,'" he complains.

But despite the modern reader's immediate bias in favor of the individual asserting his rights, we must not overlook the fact that Miller, in the course of the dramatic action and in his knowledge of late seventeenth-century Puritan society, has left a middle road open to us. In the midst of the first confrontation between Proctor and the constituted "authority" we find Rebecca Nurse, a much-respected elder in the community, who agrees with Proctor about too much mention of hell in God's church and about the dangers to the community implicit in all this talk of witchcraft. Yet, she also advises Proctor that he "cannot break charity with [his] minister," for this also leads to dangerous consequences. That Miller himself sees the wisdom of her position becomes clear in one of the expository asides in the play: "But, as in all such matters, the issue was not clear-cut, for danger was still a possibility, and in unity still lay the best promise of safety."

Since both sides—Proctor's and "authority's"—have a certain rationale to them, the confrontations within the play are more effectively presented. If, for instance, Miller allowed no room for the reasonableness of Danforth's position, no meaningful conflict between him and Hale or Proctor could develop, and the struggle which Proctor faces within himself—as will be discussed later—would be reduced significantly.

Yet, as the play develops, all assertions of theocratic control by those in power gradually lose strength. When the fear of

Salem, the fear of the approaching Chaos, leads to the peremptory condemnation of numbers of citizens on the flimsiest of evidence, there is no choice but to align oneself with the Proctors. The trials are reduced to utter absurdity when Parris affirms the "sacred purpose" of those conducting it: "We are here, your Honor, precisely to discover what no one has ever seen." Those who fear the deterioration of Order are, at first unwittingly, the primary cause of it.

Even on the simplest level of human relationships, a disintegration is evident: Ezekiel Cheever, in the holy name of the state, must violate a bond of friendship and arrest Elizabeth Proctor. His is the cry of the state pawn as he has existed from Pontius Pilate to the Nazi exterminator who refuses to become morally involved, while carrying out the letter of an obviously corrupt law. "You know yourself I must do as I'm told," he argues, ". . . believe me, Proctor, how heavy be the law, all its tonnage I do carry on my back tonight."

The crowning touch comes when Rebecca Nurse, described as "the very brick and mortar of the church," is arrested, accused of witchcraft by the decadent Abigail Williams, and condemned to be hanged. Even Hale, who first is in favor of the decision, argues that "an hour before the Devil fell, God thought him beautiful in Heaven," eventually sees that the power wielded by the evil Abbie Williams in these witch trials can lead to nothing but the chaos and desolation symbolically presented in the fourth act, with cows wandering the highroads, land fallen waste, and orphaned children stumbling aimlessly about. With the prosecution of Goody Nurse, at one time an arbiter of disputes herself, "the main role of government," as Miller explains in another expository aside, has changed "from that of arbiter to that of the scourge of God."

Perhaps by a study of the individual character of Reverend John Hale we can best see Miller's immediate tendency to "pity them all, just as we shall be pitied someday," and also understand what seems to be the playwright's ultimate condemnation of the New England theocrats. Hale honestly believes that his personal quest to hunt for witches is in the best interests of God's Kingdom and of the Salem community.

> His goal is light, goodness and its preservation, and he knows the exaltation of the blessed whose intelligence, . . . is finally called upon to face what may be a bloody fight with the Fiend himself.

The irony implicit in this slightly hyperbolic descriptive passage immediately gives us a hint that the man is one of those who could commit the most heinous crimes in the name of infinite goodness. But more important is the fact that as the play develops he comes to the realization that he had been deluded all the time he took part in the witch-hunts, that all of his work for the cause of glory had been naught — to put it in his own idiom — but Satan's handiwork.

Hale, the man who first appears on behalf of the state "weighted with authority," eventually finds the courage to "denounce these proceedings" and "quit the court." It is this growth in knowledge and the courage to act on that knowledge which set Hale apart from, and above, those in league with the theocracy in general and Danforth in particular, who by the last scene surely knows that the trials were a fraud perpetrated largely from motives of greed and vengeance — witness his desperate attempt to "smooth over" his mistake by trying to get Proctor to confess — and yet who refuses to bend from his strict authoritarian position. "Better hang innocent people than weaken the state" would not be too much an exaggeration of what he seems to contend.

The greatest dramatic confrontation in the play — the final scene between Hale and Proctor — is at least partially prepared for by the "conversion" which Hale experiences. Because Hale, an intelligent and responsible man who has recognized his own folly, is the one to "tempt" Proctor with the opportunity to escape with his life, the dramatic tension is magnified significantly. But we shall return to this after a closer look at the main character of the play.

The question which John Proctor shrieks out in anguish during the last scene of Act IV—"God in Heaven, what is John Proctor, what is John Proctor?"—is central to the individual tragedy of the protagonist. Similar to Reverend Hale, he must assess his position with reference to society and his own beliefs, and act accordingly. But with Proctor the difficulty is more complex in proportion to the added complexity of his involvement in the Salem affairs. He is caught in a web of moral dilemmas involving not only his own fate, but that of his wife, his friends, and the entire Salem community. In the larger sense, the sense that would merit calling *The Crucible* a true tragedy, John Proctor is "man" thrown into a number of situations which demand enormous moral courage to make the right choices. As the play progresses these choices grow in significance.

First, in the already discussed thematic network of the play, John Proctor is the individual who must decide whether or not he will assert himself against an overbearing authoritarian government. Although the decision involves his position in the society as a Christian, he seems to find it rather easy to break from the church (and state) when he can no longer respect the presiding minister in Salem. His loyalty to his own beliefs—which do not include "golden candlesticks" for pulpits or "hellfire" sermons—are contradicted by Reverend Parris, so he resists the reigning authority and retreats to his farm. But thus far his rebellion against the church really involves none but his own welfare, and that in no profound way.

It is not until the talk of witch-hunting becomes a reality that Proctor is forced to make a choice not entirely in his own interest. We must remember that Proctor's first reaction to the witch trials is one of mere disdain: he knows that Abigail Williams is a fraud, but does not wish to show her up as such for fear of implicating himself as a lecher, and possibly because of a dormant affection he has for her. Proctor, the man who will later call Cheever a "Pontius Pilate!" for his passive role in the proceedings, and who will also cry out to Hale—"You are a coward! Though you be ordained in God's own tears, you are a coward now!"—is first of all a coward himself. Even the insistent prodding from his wife does not move him to do his manly duty; she must be arrested before he finally takes action against Abigail. Perhaps by this point in the drama we can see John Proctor as the common man, with a natural fear of the repercussions his involvement might produce, trying to remain safely aloof from any controversial proceedings. He is only raised to greatness when actually forced into action, and even then he has a difficult time of it.

As the drama unfolds and Proctor is repeatedly forced, in spite of himself, to take significant courses of action, we can almost sense that the playwright is leading up to a final dramatic crisis in which the protagonist will have to face the ultimate decision. Whether Miller convinces us of the probability of Proctor's last choice or not is crucial to an honest judgment of the play. The choice is simply stated: will John Proctor refuse to sign a false confession and by so doing die on the gallows for the sake of a commitment to others, or will he sign to be granted a pardon. John Hale's argument heightens the difficulty of the choice because of its perfect rationality. He urges Elizabeth Proctor to induce her husband to sign:

> . . . cleave to no faith when faith brings blood. It is mistaken law that leads you to sacrifice. Life, woman, life is God's most precious gift; no principle, however glorious, may justify the taking of it. . . . Quail not before God's judgment in this, for it may well be God damns a liar less than he that throws his life away for pride.

Hale's argument is too sound to be refuted rationally, but, the *irrational* reply which Elizabeth gives — and heroism needs often be irrational — explains in part how Proctor can eventually refuse to accept it. She says, simply and quietly, "I think that be the Devil's argument." Indeed, for John Proctor, struggling within himself at every turn, it *is* the Devil's argument, the personal Devil within him, which has been tempting him from the beginning of the play to avoid any involvement in human affairs, to avoid any commitment to his fellow human beings.

The momentous self-laceration which John Proctor undergoes while trying to make his choice, faltering completely at one point in his frail human way, and only regaining his courage with the help of his wife and friends, is finally convincing because it is perfectly in character. Proctor is weak, like most men, to the very end, but he has the potential for greatness likewise common to all men. When John Proctor shouted "I am no saint," one could easily imagine Arthur Miller denying him and asserting that at one point or other in his life, whether the conditions be as trying as those in Salem or not, a man must make a commitment to humanity.

JOHN PROCTOR AND THE PROBLEM OF INVOLVEMENT AND COMMITMENT

Proctor, as a character, carries Miller's essential social message of the play. Earlier in his career, Miller was quite explicit about man's personal involvement in all of mankind. His play *All My Sons* showed the tragedy which occurs when Joe Keller tries to operate only in terms of his immediate family and refuses to acknowledge his larger obligation to all of mankind. Miller's social views include his beliefs that man cannot isolate himself from the trials of all humanity, and the man who refuses to be committed to some cause will face tragic results. If a man is to be a part of society, he must function and participate in all aspects of society. Thus, many of Miller's plays center upon the idea of commitment and involvement.

John Proctor tries to avoid any involvement in the Salem witchcraft trials. His reason for this attempt is dramatically motivated by his past folly of committing adultery with Abigail Williams. The guilt connected with this past act makes Proctor hesitant to speak openly because he would condemn himself as a lecher. Basically, then, in the first act Proctor attempts to completely separate himself from the initial proceedings, saying to Reverend Hale that he hopes the minister will restore common sense to the community. Proctor, like Pontius Pilate, tries to wash his hands of the entire affair.

For eight days, Proctor tended his farm and remained completely oblivious to the events transpiring in Salem. This refusal to acknowledge current events is abruptly brought to an end when their servant, Mary Warren, announces that she is an official of the court and that Elizabeth Proctor has been "somewhat mentioned." Proctor still wants to dismiss the hearings, but his wife uses his guilt about adultery to extract a promise that he will expose Abigail as a fraud. The point to remember is that Proctor is being forced by his wife to become involved—it is not his free and open decision.

Before Proctor is forced to make this step, Reverend Hale arrives and then, later, the man with a warrant for Elizabeth's arrest. These events force an involvement upon John Proctor, since the trials he has tried to ignore have now invaded his private sanctuary. His first step is still designed to escape commitment. He uses Mary Warren as an appeal to the law for a reversal of the court edict. Only when this fails does John Proctor take his final step and denounce Abigail as a "whore."

As a result of his involvement, John finds himself accused of being a witch. After being tried and condemned to death, John refuses to confess ("give them the lie") because of his pride and stubbornness. However, he does not want to die for such an absurd reason. He is therefore faced with the predicament of being completely against the other condemned witches, and by his confession, becoming partly responsible for the deaths of his fellow prisoners. The other course open to him is to align himself completely with the condemned witches. There is finally no middle ground left open to John Proctor. He must commit himself to one side or the other. His choice to die is a choice to commit himself to his friends and die an honest man.

THREE VIEWS OF AUTHORITY

REVEREND JOHN HALE

John Hale arrives in the village as the voice of authority about witches. He is in some sense responsible for getting the entire proceedings under way. When he first appears, he is strong and confident of his views and assured that there is an invisible world of witches which beguile mankind. He strongly advocates the authority of the church to search out and punish all the unknown enemies of the church.

Until the second act of the drama, the reader fails to make any distinction between Hale and Parris. They both seem to hold the same viewpoint. But in the second act when Hale visits the Proctor household, he is informed by Proctor of some of the actual facts in the community. At the same time, he is the witness to Elizabeth Proctor's arrest for being a witch. He knows that Elizabeth Proctor is innocent, but at this time, he is unable to set himself against the authority of the court because he has been educated to respect the authority of those above him.

In the third act, Hale begins to change. He has had faith in the honesty and integrity of John Proctor and when John makes his accusation against Abigail, only Hale sees that this accusation is made at the expense of the man's own reputation. When the court fails to accept Proctor's account of Abigail's treachery, Hale takes the first step toward asserting his own individual view of matters. He renounces the proceedings of the court and leaves.

Finally, Hale reappears as a man who is the voice of practicality. He urges the condemned to confess because life is more important than anything else. Ultimately Hale represents the switch from blind adherence to authority to independent judgment about the trials. Unfortunately, he changes too late and is rendered ineffective in saving the lives of innocent men.

JUDGE DANFORTH

It would be easy for the modern man to laugh at the position of Judge Danforth, but then, we must also recognize that there are still many men who function by the letter of the law and have no human interest in the results. Danforth is presented in terms of the ideal, staunch Puritan who believed so strongly in the *authority* of his position that any attempt to undermine his position was also an attempt to undermine the position of the entire church. Consequently, Danforth is a strict judge who can never relent on any point.

In order to prove the power of the church and ultimately the power of the authority of the church, he becomes an inhuman monster. He cannot admit that such authority as represented by his position could ever make a mistake of any kind, and consequently many innocent people were hanged simply to prove that his word was authoritative even though it was wrong.

REVEREND SAMUEL PARRIS

As Miller points out in his brief preliminary sketch of Reverend Parris, "there is very little good to be said for him." He is a man of weak moral caliber any way we look at him, concerned only with personal welfare and jealous in a petty manner about respect for his authority as minister. His role in the witch trials themselves show him as a man of little principle. At first, he is reluctant to foster any talk of witches because of the role his daughter plays in the affair. He eventually becomes one of the primary and most adamant prosecutors as a way to secure his own power in Salem.

Dramatically and thematically the character of Reverend Parris is important as he is opposed to the protagonist, John Proctor; Proctor has his first conflict with authority in the person of Reverend Parris and, ultimately, his decision to be hanged is not a victory for Parris but the symbol of the complete defeat of Parris as a man and minister.

The Historical Background

CONCEPTS OF PURITANISM IN
THE CRUCIBLE

The Puritans were a group that had suffered religious persecution in the Old World and came to America for the sole purpose
of establishing their religion in a place where they would be free
of persecution of any type. Having endured personal persecution
in England and elsewhere, the Puritans, in turn, became the per-
secutors when they arrived in America.

The unusual nature of their religion lent itself to all types of
persecution and fear of witches. The Puritans were a type who
felt that their way of life was absolutely right, and all other ways
were wrong. They would allow no person to remain in the community who was not a member in good standing with the church.
History tells us of people being driven into the wilderness when
it was revealed that they possessed a religion different from
Puritanism.

Some basic tenets of Puritanism are important to a full understanding of *The Crucible*. The first is the *Doctrine of the Elect*.
The Puritans believed that when a person is born or at any given
time later, he might be chosen by God to become one of the
Elect, that is, one of the people who would receive divine salvation. There is nothing that man himself could do to achieve this
state; instead, it was entirely predestined by God. Even though
the Puritans never emphasized it, it was assumed that those who
were not among the elect would not receive divine salvation.
The choice of who would be among the elect was completely
arbitrary and no amount of good works, righteous living, or moral
behavior could help a person achieve this status of being Elect.
This concept is also called Predestination or foreordination. An
individual could never tell whether he was among the Elect;
therefore, he lived a righteous life so as to be prepared for being
elected when the day came. It was furthermore assumed that if a

person was among the Elect, he could do no wrong. The paradox in this type of belief is that if he were actually among the Elect, he could do wrong and would still be saved because once a person is elected, then he is saved forever.

In terms of *The Crucible*, if God can then elect certain people to be saved, it was highly possible that the Devil could select certain people to be bewitched. For the Puritans, the Devil was not some abstract figure, but was a vivid and active enemy of mankind. Many stories tell of the "Black Man" who was lurking just outside the village gates or hiding in the forest waiting to trap a man and bring him into the ways of the Devil. (For an excellent presentation of this idea, see Nathaniel Hawthorne's short story "Young Goodman Brown," Appendix II.)

The Puritans accepted the story that the Devil was once one of God's angels who had fallen from grace. After being thrown from heaven for betraying God, the Devil set up a continual campaign to destroy the designs of God. This concept is used in *The Crucible* when Reverend Hale mentions that the Devil's ways are manifold and if the Devil were able to deceive God, then it would be easy for him to deceive man.

Another concept of Puritanism that is important is the view of *Theocracy*. The Puritans believed in a government that was totally controlled by the church. If a person were not a member of the church, he could not vote in elections, much less hold offices. During the earliest history of the church, the ministers were also the main officers and administrators of the civil government. Thus, if a person like John Proctor did not attend church, he could be punished and excommunicated from the church, thereby losing all of his property and rights. During the play, the fact that Proctor has not been attending church regularly is held against him as incriminating evidence. Furthermore, a man who does not know the catechism of the church also becomes suspect. Old Goody Osborne was convicted partly because she could not remember the commandments. John and Elizabeth Proctor are requested by Reverend Hale to recite their commandments. The reader should therefore realize how powerful the church was and how much authority the minister of the church wielded.

While the Puritan views about sin were strict, they also thought that every man is constantly being tempted by the Devil toward some sin. Part of the church belief was that once a man sinned he must first openly confess his sin, then repent and finally perform some act of penance. Without open confession, a person had no chance of ever being saved. Consequently, in *The Crucible* many people are ready to confess because they know that they will then be forgiven; but without confession, they stand the possibility of being hanged. It seems needless to point out the irrationality of such a view, which lent itself to many false confessions to avoid hanging.

One of the worse sins a man could commit was that of adultery. Consequently, John Proctor makes the supreme effort when he himself confesses to this most terrible sin. (Compare Hawthorne's handling of the concept of adultery in *The Scarlet Letter*.) As only Reverend Hale recognizes, Proctor must have been deeply convinced of the falsity of the children's accusation to so damn himself by such a confession.

In general, the Puritans were a sober and fearful group who felt that anything pleasant was inspired by the Devil. Women were forbidden to dress prettily; children were not expected to play games; theaters were forbidden as being the breeding place of the Devil; and dancing of any kind was a cardinal sin. Consequently, when the young children were caught dancing in the woods, they knew that they had committed a heinous sin. It is then suggested that they pretended to be under the spell of witches so as to avoid punishment. Other views could suggest that they were so deprived of all natural outlets for joy that they welcomed the opportunity to be the center of attention for a while.

PURITAN CONCEPTS OF THE DEVIL AND WITCHES FOUND IN *THE CRUCIBLE*

During the seventeenth century and well into the eighteenth century, belief in the reality of witches was widespread both in

America and in Europe. Thousands of people were executed during the period; and few people questioned the actual existence of witches. The only problem to the seventeenth-century mind was how to identify a witch.

Perhaps more than any other group, the Puritans accepted most readily the idea of witches existing in any society. Part of this results from the Puritans' complete acceptance of the contents of the Bible. They accepted every word of the Bible as totally accurate and would allow no debate on this matter. Moses' pronouncement in Exodus 22:18 "Thou shalt not suffer a witch to live" became a phrase known to almost everyone in the Puritan community. When Elizabeth and John Proctor only hint that it is not proven that witches exist, the Reverend Hale is shocked and cries out: "You surely do not fly against the Gospel, the Gospel—." In spite of advancements in science and knowledge, we see that there still existed a strong and determined belief in the reality of witches.

As indicated in the preceding section, the concept of the Devil grew out of basic tenets of the Puritan religion. The Puritans accepted completely the doctrine of original sin and many sermons emphasized that man was born depraved and sinful. He was depicted as existing on the verge of eternal damnation and was seen as a potential colleague of the Devil. Ministers delighted in telling the members of the congregation that they were worms, insects, dogs, and filthy beasts.

Some forty-five years after the Salem witchcraft trials, a famous Puritan minister, Jonathan Edwards, used the following imagery to characterize the depraved state of mankind: "The God that holds you over the pit of Hell, much as one holds a spider, or some loathsome insect, over the fire abhors you, and is dreadfully provoked; his wrath towards you burns like fire; he looks upon you as worthy of nothing else, but to be cast into the fire. . . ." It was preaching like this which prompted John Proctor to stay away from church and explain his absence as follows: "I have trouble enough without I come five mile to hear him preach only hellfire and bloody damnation. . . . Others stay away from church these days because you [Reverend Parris] hardly ever mention God any more."

Given the view that man is on the verge of damnation and is born evil and depraved, it was then easy for the Puritan to see a devil hiding behind every tree ready to trap and ensnare man. For the Puritan, the Devil did not work alone. He employed many legions of helpers which were generally referred to as witches.

The function of the Devil was to tempt men to sin and to disobey the commandments of God, and thereby he could slowly destroy God's kingdom. Since the Devil had once deceived God, it was easy for him to assume any shape on earth and deceive even the best of men. As Reverend Hale maintains: "Until an hour before the Devil fell, God thought him beautiful in Heaven." Man must therefore take every possible precaution against something so deceptive as the Devil, whose present attack seemed to be against the New World.

The Puritan felt that the Devil had concentrated all of his attention upon destroying the New World. This view is a result of the Puritan belief that their religion was the new and only religion that was approved by God and that soon there would be a New Canaan in New England. Consequently, the Devil could most effectively destroy God's purpose by attacking his new "chosen people" in the New Canaan. They also believed that the Devil held his strongest foothold in the New World because of the vast regions of forests and the vast numbers of barbarous savages existing in America. Furthermore, once the New Canaan were established, the Devil would virtually cease to exist and if he was going to destroy God's purpose, he must act quickly and attack with all his force.

Knowing that the Devil's time in which he could fulfill his destructive aims was limited, the Puritans could then readily accept the fact that he would employ legions of helpers — witches — to attack the New Canaan. They thought they had found his center of attack when they discovered so many witches in Salem,

Massachusetts, a center of Puritanism. The Reverend Hale confirms this when he says "There is a misty plot afoot so subtle we should be criminal to cling to old respects and ancient friendships." The Puritan was ready to accuse anyone of being a witch and accept anyone else's accusation, because they knew that the Devil had to employ many witches to accomplish his goal before God's kingdom was ultimately established.

What a witch actually is and how to discover one was never solved by the Puritans. The Devil used witches to help him gain his goal and a person became a witch by entering into some type of covenant with the Devil. Once a person entered into this contract with the Devil, then that person would attack other innocent people. The identification becomes more complex when we realize that a witch could be invisible and could enter a person's body without that person knowing it.

Additional difficulties arise in discovering a witch when we realize that the Puritan also believed that the Devil or one of his agents could assume the shape of an innocent person and then torment another person. The tormented person then would automatically accuse the innocent person of being a witch and this innocent person would be punished for being in league with the Devil. By this subtle means, the Devil would gain his end of tormenting an innocent person and of bringing confusion into God's world.

By an equally strange quirk of logic, once a person confessed to being a witch, then the person was free. This accords with the Puritan view that salvation begins by making an open confession of one's sins. Yet if a person were actually a witch, he would have no qualms about lying and could therefore confess to repentance so as to continue doing the Devil's work. Yet, one faction thought that if a witch confessed, then his soul could be saved; whereas another faction contended that to confess to being a witch would eternally damn a person. Rebecca Nurse refused to confess because she felt that such a confession would eternally damn her.

In conclusion, there was much confusion and disagreement about how to detect a witch and just what a witch actually was. The Puritans agreed only that witches came from the invisible world and sought for some means of making them known to the visible world so as to destroy them. In their attempt many innocent persons lost their lives.

A BRIEF VIEW OF THE SALEM WITCHCRAFT TRIALS

Prior to February, 1692, the town of Salem was beset by many internal trials and difficulties. Since the town functioned chiefly around the church, dissension within the congregation about the election of Reverend Parris caused factions to develop. Reverend Parris had apparently been elected minister without a firm majority, and accusations of preferment were constantly made. Parris did not help matters by demanding a title to the minister's home, requesting that large expenditures be made for the church, and quarreling over who should supply his firewood.

Without any definite boundaries set in the New World, a quarrel had prevailed for a long time between the Putnams and the Nurses, two of the more influential families of the community. Wills, deeds, and lawsuits were constantly being filed and one neighbor was constantly bickering with another about some minor point of law.

When the Reverend Parris came to Salem, he brought with him a Negro servant, Tituba, whose ways were strange and foreign to the grim Puritans. When it was discovered that Tituba had been teaching Reverend Parris' eleven-year-old daughter, Elizabeth, and her cousin, Abigail, about palmistry, the thought of witchcraft became widespread. Then, in February, 1692, when Betty Parris began having some type of fits and acted in an afflicted manner, and when the doctors could not find any natural cause for her actions, it was suggested that they search for things unnatural as the cause of her illness.

Palmistry, or forecasting the future, was considered a crime by the Puritans, as it was in many other branches of Christianity. Miller, however, changes this aspect of history and has the girls dancing in the nearby forests. The dancing has more dramatic appeal than does palmistry and serves to heighten the dramatic conflicts.

The Reverend Parris sent for some of his fellow ministers, and he hoped to keep the entire affair secret. But before long, it became public knowledge. Exactly what happened next is not known for certain.

On February 29, 1692, the first three warrants for arrest were issued. The three accused of being witches were the ones who would most likely fit the role. Tituba was a Negro who had practiced palmistry, a sin in the Puritan eyes. Sarah Good was a disreputable old woman who wandered through the streets begging and smoking a pipe. Sarah Osborne had committed the sin of failing to attend church regularly and was suspected of other immoral acts. When the first confession was extracted, others were named and arrested.

Before the trials were over, nineteen people were hanged as witches, Giles Corey was pressed to death for refusing to answer to an indictment, and two dogs were also hanged for witchcraft. During the trials, fifty-five people openly confessed to being witches, and at the end of the executions, many people were in jail either awaiting trial or condemned to die at a future date.

During the trials when anyone contested the action of the court, the judges could easily point to the confessions already extracted. Unfortunately, the trials took place while the governor of the colony had to be away on a campaign against the Indians. In his absence he appointed the lieutenant-governor (William Stroughton) as chief justice. During the trials, great attention was given to the young girls who said that they were afflicted by witches. Stroughton was a firm believer in witches and highly orthodox in his religious beliefs. He seemed to be a man who could not stand any reflection on his authority. It was he who issued the first death warrant and who saw to it that the sentence was carried out.

The trial began in February and in addition to the one witch executed in June, five were hanged on July 19, five on August 19, and eight more on September 22. On October 29, due to various pressures, Governor Phips dismissed the court and there were ultimately no more hangings. But at this time, there were still one hundred and fifty "witches" who had been legally arrested and had not been brought to trial.

The presence of this large number of people accused of being witches awaiting to be tried contributed to the cessation of the witch trials. Governor Phips ordered the court to devise a more reliable method of determining whether or not a person was a witch than by accepting the phantasmal evidence of the young girls. This order brought together many of the minds of New England and finally some of the ministers spoke out against accepting spectral evidence or the confessions of the accused.

Also by this time, too many respectable people had been accused of being witches so that no one was safe anymore. This excessive accusation contributed strongly to undermining the validity of the trials. Added to this was the rumor that some wives of important men were actually accused and not arrested and that some men were able to bribe the court. In other words, many circumstances ultimately combined to bring the hearings to a close.

The Salem witchcraft trials did not end with the cessation of the trial itself. Only three years later, certain individuals connected with the event began to retract. By 1709, heirs of the accused began to petition the government for redress, and in 1711, various sums of money were awarded to certain descendants of the people hanged as witches, along with complete reinstatement of the accuseds' reputation.

McCARTHYISM AND *THE CRUCIBLE*

In 1950, America was involved in a great struggle with Russia. In the throes of the cold war and with fears that Communism was threatening all aspects of American life, with the memory of World War II still fresh, and with the dread of another and greater conflict with Soviet Russia, America had a secret and unexpressed fear of this alien land populated by people whose political ideology was so incompatible with the American way of life.

In Wheeling, West Virginia, in 1950, an almost totally unknown senator was catapulted into national notoriety when he casually accused the Democratic administration of harboring and supporting Communists in the American government. The past years under Democratic leaders had been "twenty years of treason," under the "idiocy of a Truman, rotted by the deceit of an Acheson, corrupted by red slime of a White." It seems useless to point out that such language is not that used by a reasonable person and could easily offer itself for comparison to the absurd charges leveled by the children of Salem.

America, out of fear, fell prey to the ridiculous charges made by McCarthy and entered into a period, similar to that in Salem, when the rational mind was affected by fear. Even high leaders in the government could not act freely without taking into consideration the effect it might have on McCarthy's investigations. The more liberal faction of the American government began appropriately to label McCarthy's activities as "witch-hunts." Miller uses the famous McCarthy saying in his play; the senator often maintained that those who opposed his hearings were Communists, and consequently, any public official who offered criticism of the hearings soon found himself defending himself against the charge of being a part of a Communist conspiracy. Too large a segment of the American public was ready to accept these false and irrational charges, so that after a short time, the effectiveness of the American government was seriously hampered.

Miller uses only the broad general analogies to the McCarthy hearings. Anyone who opposed the authority of the Salem judges was automatically suspected of trying to undermine the court in the same way McCarthy accused anyone who opposed him of being a Communist. Furthermore, the general atmosphere of suspicion aroused by the McCarthy hearings is analogous to the panic and fear caused by the accusations of the tormented Salem girls.

When *The Crucible* was first produced, many critics saw in it only the analogies to the McCarthy hearings and did not look beyond this level of interpretation. Now that these hearings are something of the past, we can re-evaluate the play and discover that it possesses the innate qualities which make for significant drama, and also realize that the relationship of the McCarthy hearings are significant only in the broadest and most general **terms.**

Review Questions and Essay Topics

1. Reverend Hale arrives in Salem as an *Authority* on witches but by the end of the play has changed so completely that he wants the condemned to make false confessions to save themselves. Show how this reversal is dramatically motivated.

2. In the second act, Elizabeth Proctor acts as a judge of her husband's behavior, but in the final scene when she could save his life, she refuses to judge him. Justify her refusal to judge her husband's final decision.

3. How much is John's past adultery with Abigail Williams responsible for Elizabeth and John's being accused as witches?

4. How does Reverend Hale's final plea affect John Proctor's decision. Why does he even appear in the final act?

5. Show how Danforth is a good man who is blinded by the authority invested in him.

6. What is Giles Corey's function in the play?

7. Danforth makes the statement: "Either you are with this court or you are against it." Would Miller agree with this statement? Is there a middle ground which the average citizen can take?

8. How is Abigail Williams presented as the most evil force in the play?

9. Is John Proctor's decision to die believable? Justify his decision in terms of commitment to his fellow prisoners.

10. Discuss the Parris-Proctor conflict in terms of the individual versus authority.

Historical Documents from the Salem Witchcraft Trials

NOTE: The following excerpts are reprinted from *Records of Salem Witchcraft*, 1864, edited by William E. Woodward. There has been no attempt to change the language of the original documents; punctuation and capitals have been left exactly as they appear in the original documents.

SARAH GOOD

Warrant vs. Sarah Good.

Salem February the 29th 1692
To Constable George Locker.

Whereas Messrs. Joseph Hutchinson, Thomas Putnam, Edward Putnam, and Thomas Preston, Yeomen of Salem Village in the County of Essex, personally appeared before us and made Complaint on Behalf of their Majesties against Sarah Good the wife of William Good of Salem Village abovesaid for suspicion of Witchcraft by her Committed, and thereby much Injury done by Eliz. Parris, Abigail Williams, Ann Putnam and Elizabeth Hubbard all of Salem Village aforesaid Sundry times within this two months and Lately also done, at Salem Village Contrary to the peace of our Sovereign Lord and Lady William & Mary, King & Queen of England etc. — You are therefore in their Majesties' names hereby required to apprehend & bring before us, the said Sarah Good tomorrow about ten of the clock in the forenoon at the house of Lt Nathaniel Ingersoll in Salem Village or as soon as may be then and there to be Examined Relating to the abovesaid premises and hereof you are not to fail at your peril.

Dated. Salem, february 29th 1692

John Hathorne }
Jonathan Corwin } Assistants.

Examination of Sarah Good.

The examination of Sarah Good before the worshipful Assistants John Hathorne Jonathan Corwin.

Q. Sarah Good what evil Spirit have you familiarity with

A. None

Q. Have you made no contract with the devil

Good answered no.

Q. Why do you hurt these children

A. I do not hurt them. I scorn it.

Q. Who do you employ then to do it.

A. I employ nobody

Q. What creature do you employ then.

A. no creature but I am falsely accused.

Q. Why did you go away muttering from Mr Parris his house.

A. I did not mutter but I thanked him for what he gave my child.

Q. have you made no contract with the devil.

A. no.

Hathorne desired the children all of them to look upon her and see if this were the person that had hurt them and so they all did look upon her, and said this was one of the persons that did torment them — presently they were all tormented.

Q. Sarah Good do you not see now what you have done, why do you not tell us the truth, why do you thus torment these poor children

A. I do not torment them.

Q. who do you employ then.

A. I employ nobody I scorn it.

Q. how came they thus tormented

A. what do I know you bring others here and now you charge me with it.

Q. why who was it.

A. I do not know but it was some you brought into the meeting house with you.

Q. we brought you into the meeting house.

A. but you brought in two more.

Q. who was it then that tormented the children.

A. it was osborne.

Q. what is it you say when you go muttering away from person's houses

A. if I must tell I will tell.

Q. do tell us then

A. if I must tell, I will tell, it is the commandments. I may say my commandments I hope.

56

Q. what commandment is it.
A. if I must tell I will tell, it is a psalm.
Q. what psalm.
after a long time she muttered over some part of a psalm.
Q. who do you serve
A. I serve God
Q. what God do you serve.
A. the God that made heaven and earth. though she was not willing to mention the word God. her answers were in a very wicked spiteful manner. reflecting and retorting against the authority with base and abusive words and many lies she was taken in it was here said that her husband had said that he was afraid that she either was a witch or would be one very quickly. the worshipful Mr. Hawthorne asked him his reason why he said so of her, whether he had ever seen anything of her, he answered no, not in this nature, but it was her bad carriage to him, and indeed said he I may say with tears that she is an enemy to all good.

Salem Village March the 1st 1692

Written by Ezekiel Cheever . . .

Dated Salem March 29th 1692

Sarah Good upon Examination denieth the matter of fact (viz) that she ever used any witchcraft or hurt the abovesaid children or any of them.
The above-named Children being all present positively accused her of hurting of them Sundry times within this two months and also that morning.
Sarah Good being Asked if, that she did not then hurt them who did it. And the children being again tortured she looked upon them And said that it was one of them we brought into the house with us. We asked her who it was, she then Answered and said it was Sarah Osborne, and Sarah Osborne was then under Custody and not in the house; And the children being quickly after recovered out of their fit said that it was Sarah Good and also Sarah Osborne that then did hurt & torment or afflict them—although both of them at the same time at a distance or Remote from them personally—there were also sundry other Questions put to her and Answers given thereunto by her according as is also given in.

John Hathorne }
Jonathan Corwin } Assistants.

Examination of Tituba Indian.

The examination of Tituba.

Q. Tituba what evil spirit have you familiarity with.

A. none.

Q. why do you hurt these children.

A. I do not hurt them.

Q. who is it then.

A. the devil for aught I know.

Q. Did you never see the devil.

A. The devil came to me and bid me serve him.

Q. Who have you seen.

A. Four women sometimes hurt the children.

Q. Who were they.

A. Goody Osborne and Sarah Good and I do not know who the other were. Sarah Good and Osborne would have me hurt the children but I would not she further saith there was a tall man of Boston that she did see.

Q. when did you see them.

A Last night at Boston.

Q. what did they say to you.

A. they said hurt the children

Q. and did you hurt them

A. no there is 4 women and one man they hurt the children and they lay all upon me and they tell me if I will not hurt the children they will hurt me.

Q. but did you not hurt them

A. yes, but I will hurt them no more.

Q. are you not sorry you did hurt them.

A. yes.

Q. and why then do you hurt them.

A. they say hurt children or we will do worse to you.

Q. what have you seen.

A. an man come to me and say serve me.

Q. what service.

A. hurt the children and last night there was an appearance that said kill the children and if I would no[t] go on hurting the children they would do worse to me.

Q. what is this appearance you see.

A. Sometimes it is like a hog and sometimes like a great dog, this appearance she saith she did see 4 times.

Q. what did it say to you

A. it . . . the black dog said serve me but I said I am afraid he said if I did not he would do worse to me.

Q. what did you say to it.

A. I will serve you no longer. then he said he would hurt me and then he looked like a man and threatens to hurt me, she said that this man had a yellow bird that kept with him and he told me he had more pretty things that he would give me if I would serve him.

Q. what were these pretty things.

A. he did not show me them.

Q. what also have you seen

A. two rats, a red rat and a black rat.

Q. what did they say to you.

A. they said serve me.

Q. when did you see them.

A. last night and they said serve me, but I said I would not

Q. what service.

A. she said hurt the children.

Q. did you not pinch Elizabeth Hubbard this morning

A. the man brought her to me and made me pinch her

Q. why did you go to Thomas Putnam's last night and hurt his child.

A. they pull and haul me and make me go

Q. and what would have you do.

A. Kill her with a knife.

Lieutenant Fuller and others said at this time when the child saw these persons and was tormented by them that she did complain of a knife, that they would have her cut her head off with a knife.

Q. how did you go

A. we ride upon sticks and are there presently.

Q. why did you not tell your master.

A. I was afraid they said they would cut off my head if I told.

Q. would you not have hurt others if you could.

A. They said they would hurt others but they could not

Q. what attendants hath Sarah Good.

A. a yellow bird and she would have given me one

Q. what meat did she give it

A. it did suck her between her fingers.

Q. did not you hurt Mr Currin's child

A. goody good and goody Osborne told that they did hurt Mr Currin's child and would have had me hurt him too, but I did not.

Q. what hath Sarah Osborne.

A. yellow dog, she had a thing with a head like a woman with 2 legs, and wings. Abigail Williams that lives with her Uncle Parris said that she did see the same creature, and it turned into the shape of Goody Osborne.

Q. what else have you seen with Osborne.

A. another thing, hairy it goes upright like a man it hath only 2 legs.

Q. did you not see Sarah Good upon Elizabeth Hubbard, last Saturday.

A. I did see her set a wolf upon her to afflict her, the persons with this maid did say that she did complain of a wolf.

. . . she further saith that she saw a cat with good at another time.

Q. What clothes doth the man go in

A. he goes in black clothes a tall man with white hair I think

Q. How doth the woman go

A. in a white hood and a black hood with a top knot

Q. do you see who it is that torments these children now.

A. yes it is Goody Good, she hurts them in her own shape

Q. and who is it that hurts them now.

A. I am blind now. I cannot see.

Salem Village
March the 1st 1692

Written by Ezekiel Cheever
Salem Village March 1st 1692

JOHN PROCTOR

Mary Warren's Examination

Q. Whether you did not know that it was the Devil's book when you signed.

A. I did not know it then but I know it now to be sure it was the Devil's book, in the first place to be sure I did set my hand to the devil's book: I have considered of it since you were here last and it was the devil's book that my Master Proctor brought to me and he told me if I would set my hand to that book I should believe and I did set my hand to it but...it was done with my finger. he brought the book and told me if I would take the book and touch it that I should be well and I thought then that it was the Devil's book.

Q. Was there not your consent to hurt the children when you were hurt? and said if you are afflicted I wish they were more afflicted and you and all: I said Master what makes you say so. He answered, because you go to bring out Innocent persons, I told him that that could not be. and whether the Devil took advantage at that I know not to afflict them and one night talking about them I said I did not care though they were tormented if ye charged me.

Q. Did you ever see any puppets?

A. Yes once I saw one made of cloth in Mistress Proctor's hand.

Q. Who was it like, or which of the Children was it for?

A. I cannot tell, whether for Ann Putnam or Abigail Williams for one of them it was I am sure, it was in my mistress's hand.

Q. What did you stick into the puppet?
A. I did stick in a pin about the neck of it as it was in Proctor's hand.
Q. How many more did you see afterwards?
A. I do not remember that ever I saw any more.

Mary Warren v. John Proctor.

The deposition of Mary Warren aged 20 years he[re] testifieth. I have seen the apparition of John Proctor senior among the witches and he hath often tortured me by pinching me and biting me and choking me, and pressing me on my Stomach till the blood came out of my mouth and also I saw him torture Mis Pope and Mercy lewis and John Indian upon the day of his examination and he hath also tempted me to write in his book. and to eat bread which he brought to me, which I refusing to do, Jno Proctor did most grievously torture me with variety of tortures, almost Ready to kill me.

Mary Warren owned the above
written upon her oath before and
unto the Grand Inquest on the
30 Day of June 1692

APPENDIX II

Young Goodman Brown

BY NATHANIEL HAWTHORNE

NOTE: The following story by Nathaniel Hawthorne, published in 1835, offers some interesting comparisons and contrasts to Arthur Miller's treatment of witchcraft. The imagined time in this story is shortly *before* the Salem witchcraft trials; and Hawthorne, like Miller, uses some historical names connected with the trials. For example, Goody Cloyse, Martha Carrier, and Goody Cory (Miller spells the name "Corey") were among those convicted of witchcraft.

Young Goodman Brown came forth at sunset into the street at Salem village; but put his head back, after crossing the threshold, to exchange a parting kiss with his young wife. And Faith, as the wife was aptly named, thrust her own pretty head into the street, letting the wind play with the pink ribbons of her cap while she called to Goodman Brown.

"Dearest heart," whispered she, softly and rather sadly, when her lips were close to his ear, "prithee put off your journey until sunrise and sleep in your own bed tonight. A lone woman is troubled with such dreams and such thoughts that she's afeared of herself sometimes. Pray tarry with me this night, dear husband, of all nights in the year."

"My love and my Faith," replied young Goodman Brown, "of all nights in the year, this one night must I tarry away from thee. My journey, as thou callest it, forth and back again, must needs be done 'twixt now and sunrise. What, my sweet, pretty wife, dost thou doubt me already, and we but three months married?"

"Then God bless you!" said Faith, with the pink ribbons; "and may you find all well when you come back."

"Amen!" cried Goodman Brown. "Say thy prayers, dear Faith, and go to bed at dusk, and no harm will come to thee."

So they parted; and the young man pursued his way until, being about to turn the corner by the meetinghouse, he looked back and saw the head of Faith still peeping after him with a melancholy air, in spite of her pink ribbons.

"Poor little Faith!" thought he, for his heart smote him. "What a wretch am I to leave her on such an errand! She talks of dreams, too. Methought as she spoke there was trouble in her face, as if a dream had warned her what work is to be done tonight. But no, no; 'twould kill her to think it. Well, she's a blessed angel on earth; and after this one night I'll cling to her skirts and follow her to heaven."

With this excellent resolve for the future, Goodman Brown felt himself justified in making more haste on his present evil purpose. He had taken a dreary road, darkened by all the gloomiest trees of the forest, which barely stood aside to let the narrow path creep through, and closed immediately behind. It was all as lonely as could be; and there is this peculiarity in such solitude, that the traveler knows not who may be concealed by the innumerable trunks and the thick boughs overhead; so that with lonely footsteps he may yet be passing through an unseen multitude.

"There may be a devilish Indian behind every tree," said Goodman Brown to himself; and he glanced fearfully behind him as he added, "What if the devil himself should be at my very elbow!"

His head being turned back, he passed a crook of the road, and looking forward again, beheld the figure of a man, in grave and decent attire, seated at the foot of an old tree. He arose at Goodman Brown's approach and walked onward side by side with him.

"You are late, Goodman Brown," said he. "The clock of the Old South was striking as I came through Boston, and that is full fifteen minutes agone."

"Faith kept me back a while," replied the young man, with a tremor in his voice, caused by the sudden appearance of his companion, though not wholly unexpected.

It was now deep dusk in the forest, and deepest in that part of it where these two were journeying. As nearly as could be discerned, the second traveler was about fifty years old, apparently in the same rank of life as Goodman Brown, and bearing a considerable resemblance to him, though perhaps more in expression than features. Still they might have been taken for father and son. And yet, though the elder person was as simply clad as the younger, and as simple in manner too, he had an indescribable air of one who knew the world, and who would not have felt abashed at the governor's dinner table or in King William's court, were it possible that his affairs should call him thither. But the only thing about him that could be fixed upon as remarkable was his staff, which bore the likeness of a great black snake, so curiously wrought that it might almost be seen to twist and wriggle itself like a living serpent. This, of course, must have been an ocular deception, assisted by the uncertain light.

"Come, Goodman Brown," cried his fellow traveler, "this is a dull pace for the beginning of a journey. Take my staff, if you are so soon weary."

"Friend," said the other, exchanging his slow pace for a full stop, "having kept covenant by meeting thee here, it is my purpose now to return whence I came. I have scruples touching the matter thou wot'st of."

"Sayest thou so?" replied he of the serpent, smiling apart. "Let us walk on, nevertheless, reasoning as we go; and if I convince thee not thou shalt turn back. We are but a little way in the forest yet."

"Too far! too far!" exclaimed the goodman, unconsciously resuming his walk. "My father never went into the woods on such an errand, nor his father before him. We have been a race of honest men and good Christians since the days of the martyrs; and shall I be the first of the name of Brown that ever took this path and kept" —

"Such company, thou wouldst say," observed the elder person, interpreting his pause. "Well said, Goodman Brown! I have been as well acquainted with your family as with ever a one among the Puritans; and that's no trifle to say. I helped your grandfather, the constable, when he lashed the Quaker woman so smartly through the streets of Salem; and it was I that brought your father a pitch-pine knot, kindled at my own heart, to set fire to an Indian village, in King Philip's war. They were my good friends, both; and many a pleasant walk have we had along this path, and returned merrily after midnight. I would fain be friends with you for their sake."

"If it be as thou sayest," replied Goodman Brown, "I marvel they never spoke of these matters; or, verily, I marvel not, seeing that the least rumor of the sort would have driven them from New England. We are a people of prayer, and good works to boot, and abide no such wickedness."

"Wickedness or not," said the traveler with the twisted staff, "I have a very general acquaintance here in New England. The deacons of many a church have drunk the communion wine with me; the selectmen of divers towns make me their chairman; and a majority of the Great and General Court are firm supporters of my interest. The governor and I, too — But these are state secrets."

"Can this be so?" cried Goodman Brown, with a stare of amazement at his undisturbed companion. "Howbeit, I have nothing to do with the governor and council; they have their own ways, and are no rule for a simple husbandman like me. But, were I to go on with thee, how should I meet the eye of that good old man, our minister, at Salem village? Oh, his voice would make me tremble both Sabbath day and lecture day."

Thus far the elder traveler had listened with due gravity; but now burst into a fit of irrepressible mirth, shaking himself so violently that his snake-like staff actually seemed to wriggle in sympathy.

"Ha! ha! ha!" shouted he again and again; then composing himself, "Well, go on, Goodman Brown, go on; but prithee, don't kill me with laughing."

"Well, then, to end the matter at once," said Goodman Brown, considerably nettled, "there is my wife, Faith. It would break her dear little heart; and I'd rather break my own."

"Nay, if that be the case," answered the other, "e'en go thy ways, Goodman Brown. I would not for twenty old women like the one hobbling before us that Faith should come to any harm."

As he spoke he pointed the staff at a female figure on the path, in whom Goodman Brown recognized a very pious and exemplary dame, who had taught him his catechism in youth, and was still his moral and spiritual adviser, jointly with the minister and Deacon Gookin.

"A marvel, truly, that Goody Cloyse should be so far in the wilderness at nightfall," said he. "But with your leave, friend, I shall take a cut through the woods until we have left this Christian woman behind. Being a stranger to you, she might ask whom I was consorting with and whither I was going."

"Be it so," said his fellow traveler. "Betake you to the woods, and let me keep the path."

Accordingly the young man turned aside, but took care to watch his companion, who advanced softly along the road until he had come within a staff's length of the old dame. She meanwhile, was making the best of her way, with singular speed for so aged a woman, and mumbling some indistinct words — a prayer, doubtless — as she went. The traveler put forth his staff and touched her withered neck with what seemed the serpent's tail.

"The devil!" screamed the pious old lady.

"Then Goody Cloyse knows her old friend?" observed the traveler, confronting her and leaning on his writhing stick.

"Ah, forsooth, and is it your worship indeed?" cried the good dame. "Yea, truly is it, and in the very image of my old gossip, Goodman Brown, the grandfather of the silly fellow that now is. But — would your worship believe it? — my broomstick hath strangely disappeared, stolen, as I suspect, by that unhanged witch, Goody Cory, and that, too, when I was all anointed with the juice of small-age, and cinquefoil, and wolf's bane" —

"Mingled with fine wheat and the fat of a newborn babe," said the shape of old Goodman Brown.

"Ah, your worship knows the recipe," cried the old lady, cackling aloud. "So, as I was saying, being all ready for the meeting, and no horse to ride on, I made up my mind to foot it; for they tell me there is a nice young man to be taken into communion tonight. But now your good worship will lend me your arm, and we shall be there in a twinkling."

"That can hardly be," answered her friend. "I may not spare you my arm, Goody Cloyse; but here is my staff, if you will."

So saying, he threw it down at her feet, where, perhaps, it assumed life, being one of the rods which its owner had formerly lent to the Egyptian magi. Of this fact, however, Goodman Brown could not take cognizance. He had cast up his eyes in astonishment, and, looking down again, beheld neither Goody Cloyse nor the serpentine staff, but his fellow traveler alone, who waited for him as calmly as if nothing had happened.

"That old woman taught me my catechism," said the young man; and there was a world of meaning in this simple comment.

They continued to walk onward, while the elder traveler exhorted his companion to make good speed and persevere in the path, discoursing so aptly that his arguments seemed rather to spring up in the bosom of his auditor than to be suggested by himself. As they went, he plucked a branch of maple to serve for a walking stick, and began to strip it of the twigs and little boughs, which were wet with evening dew. The moment his fingers touched them they became strangely withered and dried up as with a week's sunshine. Thus the pair proceeded, at a good free pace, until suddenly, in a gloomy hollow of the road, Goodman Brown sat himself down on the stump of a tree and refused to go any farther.

"Friend," said he, stubbornly, "my mind is made up. Not another step will I budge on this errand. What if a wretched old woman do choose to go to the devil when I thought she was going to heaven: is that any reason why I should quit my dear Faith and go after her?"

"You will think better of this by and by," said his acquaintance, composedly, "Sit here and rest yourself a while; and when you feel like moving again, there is my staff to help you along."

Without more words, he threw his companion the maple stick, and was as speedily out of sight as if he had vanished into the deepening gloom. The young man sat a few moments by the roadside, applauding himself greatly, and thinking with how clear a conscience he should meet the minister in his morning walk, nor shrink from the eye of good old Deacon Gookin. And what calm sleep would be his that very night, which was to have been spent so wickedly, but so purely and sweetly now, in the arms of Faith! Amidst these pleasant and praiseworthy meditations, Goodman Brown heard the tramp of horses along the road, and deemed it advisable to conceal himself within the verge of the forest, conscious of the guilty purpose that had brought him thither, though now so happily turned from it.

On came the hoof tramps and the voices of the riders, two grave old voices, conversing soberly as they drew near. These mingled sounds appeared to pass along the road, within a few yards of the young man's hiding place; but, owing doubtless to the depth of the gloom at that particular spot, neither the travelers nor their steeds were visible. Though their figures brushed the small boughs by the wayside, it could not be seen that they intercepted, even for a moment, the faint gleam from the strip of bright sky athwart which they must have passed. Goodman Brown alternately crouched and stood on tiptoe, pulling aside the branches and thrusting forth his head as far as he durst without discerning so much as a shadow. It vexed him the more, because he could have sworn, were such a thing possible, that he recognized the voices of the minister and Deacon Gookin, jogging along quietly, as they were wont to do, when bound to some ordination or ecclesiastical council. While yet within hearing, one of the riders stopped to pluck a switch.

"Of the two, reverend sir," said the voice like the deacon's, "I had rather miss an ordination dinner than tonight's meeting. They tell me that some of our community are to be here from Falmouth and beyond, and others from Connecticut and Rhode Island, besides several of the Indian powwows, who, after their fashion, know almost as much deviltry as the best of us. Moreover, there is a goodly young woman to be taken into communion."

"Mighty well, Deacon Gookin!" replied the solemn old tones of the minister. "Spur up, or we shall be late. Nothing can be done, you know, until I get on the ground."

The hoofs clattered again; and the voices, talking so strangely in the empty air, passed on through the forest, where no church had ever been gathered or solitary Christian prayed. Whither, then, could these holy men be journeying so deep into the heathen wilderness? Young Goodman Brown caught hold of a tree for support, being ready to sink down on the ground, faint and overburdened with the heavy sickness of his heart. He looked up to the sky, doubting whether there really was a heaven above him. Yet there was the blue arch, and the stars brightening in it.

"With heaven above and Faith below, I will yet stand firm against the devil!" cried Goodman Brown.

While he still gazed upward into the deep arch of the firmament and had lifted his hands to pray, a cloud, though no wind was stirring, hurried across the zenith and hid the brightening stars. The blue sky was still visible, except directly overhead, where this black mass of cloud was sweeping swiftly northward. Aloft in the air, as if from the depths of the cloud, came a confused and doubtful sound of voices. Once the listener fancied that he could distinguish the accents of townspeople of his own, men and women, both pious and ungodly, many of whom he had met at the communion table, and had seen others rioting at the tavern. The next moment, so indistinct were the sounds, he doubted whether he had heard aught but the murmur of the old forest, whispering without a wind. Then came a stronger swell of those familiar tones, heard daily in the sunshine at Salem village, but never until now from a cloud of night. There was one voice, of a young woman, uttering lamentations, yet with an uncertain sorrow, and entreating for some favor, which, perhaps, it would grieve her to obtain; and all the unseen multitude, both saints and sinners, seemed to encourage her onward.

"Faith!" shouted Goodman Brown, in a voice of agony and desperation; and the echoes of the forest mocked him, crying, "Faith! Faith!" as if bewildered wretches were seeking her all through the wilderness.

The cry of grief, rage, and terror was yet piercing the night, when the unhappy husband held his breath for a response. There was a scream, drowned immediately in a louder murmur of voices, fading into far-off laughter, as the dark cloud swept away, leaving the clear and silent sky above Goodman Brown. But something fluttered lightly down through the air and caught on the branch of a tree. The young man seized it, and beheld a pink ribbon.

"My Faith is gone!" cried he, after one stupefied moment. "There is no good on earth; and sin is but a name. Come, devil; for to thee is this world given."

And, maddened with despair, so that he laughed loud and long, did Goodman Brown grasp his staff and set forth again, at such a rate that he seemed to fly along the forest path rather than to walk or run. The road grew wilder and drearier and more faintly traced, and vanished at length, leaving him in the heart of the dark wilderness, still rushing onward with the instinct that guides mortal man to evil. The whole forest was peopled with frightful sounds—the creaking of the trees, the howling of wild beasts, and the yell of Indians while sometimes the wind tolled like a distant church bell, and sometimes gave a broad roar around the traveler, as if all Nature were laughing him to scorn. But he was himself the chief horror of the scene, and shrank not from its other horrors.

"Ha! ha! ha!" roared Goodman Brown when the wind laughed at him. "Let us hear which will laugh loudest. Think not to frighten me with your deviltry. Come witch, come wizard, come Indian powwow, come devil himself, and here comes Goodman Brown. You may as well fear him as he fear you."

In truth, all through the haunted forest there could be nothing more frightful than the figure of Goodman Brown. On he flew among the black pines, brandishing his staff with frenzied gestures, now giving vent to an inspiration of horrid blasphemy, and now shouting forth such laughter as set all the echoes of the forest laughing like demons around him. The fiend in his own shape is less hideous than when he rages in the breast of man. Thus sped the demoniac on his course, until, quivering among the trees, he saw a red light before him, as when the felled trunks and branches of a clearing have been set on fire, and throw up their lurid blaze against the sky, at the hour of midnight. He paused, in a lull of the tempest that had driven him onward, and heard the swell of what seemed a hymn, rolling solemnly from a distance with the weight of many voices. He knew the tune; it was a familiar one in the choir of the village meetinghouse. The verse died heavily away, and was lengthened by a chorus, not of human voices, but of all the sounds of the benighted wilderness pealing in awful harmony together. Goodman Brown cried out, and his cry was lost to his own ear by its unison with the cry of the desert.

In the interval of silence he stole forward until the light glared full upon his eyes. At one extremity of an open space, hemmed in by the dark wall of forest, arose a rock, bearing some rude, natural resemblance either to an altar or a pulpit, and surrounded by four blazing pines, their tops aflame, their stems untouched, like candles at an evening meeting. The mass of foliage that had overgrown the summit of the rock was all on fire, blazing high into the night and fitfully illuminating the whole field. Each pendent twig and leafy festoon was in a blaze. As the red light arose and fell, a numerous congregation alternately shone forth, then disappeared in shadow, and again grew, as it were, out of the darkness, peopling the heart of the solitary woods at once.

"A grave and dark-clad company," quoth Goodman Brown.

In truth they were such. Among them, quivering to and fro between gloom and splendor, appeared faces that would be seen next day at the council board of the province, and others which, Sabbath after Sabbath, looked devoutly heavenward, and benignantly over the crowded pews, from the holiest pulpits in the land. Some affirm that the lady of the governor was there. At least there were high dames well known to her, and wives of honored husbands, and widows, a great multitude, and ancient maidens, all of excellent repute, and fair young girls, who trembled lest their mothers should espy them. Either the sudden gleams of light flashing over the obscure field bedazzled Goodman Brown, or he recognized a score of the church members of Salem village famous for their especial sanctity. Good old Deacon Gookin had arrived, and waited at the skirts of that venerable saint, his revered pastor. But, irreverently consorting with these grave, reputable, and pious people, these elders of the church, these chaste dames and dewy virgins, there were men of disolute lives and women of spotted fame, wretches given over to all mean and filthy vice, and suspected even of horrid crimes. It was strange to see that the good shrank not from the wicked, nor were the sinners abashed by the saints. Scattered also among their pale-faced enemies were the Indian priests, or powwows, who had often scared their native forest with more hideous incantations than any known to English witchcraft.

"But where is Faith?" thought Goodman Brown; and, as hope came into his heart, he trembled.

Another verse of the hymn arose, a slow and mournful strain, such as the pious love, but joined to words which expressed all that our nature can conceive of sin, and darkly hinted at far more. Unfathomable to mere mortals is the lore of fiends. Verse after verse was sung; and still the chorus of the desert swelled between like the deepest tone of a mighty organ; and with the final peal of that dreadful anthem there came a sound, as if the roaring wind, the rushing streams, the howling beasts, and every other voice of the unconcerted wilderness were mingling and according with the voice of guilty man in homage to the prince of all. The four blazing pines threw up a loftier flame, and obscurely discovered shapes and visages of horror on the smoke wreaths above the impious assembly. At the same moment the fire on the rock shot redly forth and formed a glowing arch above its base, where now appeared a figure. With reverence be it spoken, the figure bore no slight similitude, both in garb and manner, to some grave divine of the New England churches.

"Bring forth the converts!" cried a voice that echoed through the field and rolled into the forest.

At the word, Goodman Brown stepped forth from the shadow of the trees and approached the congregation, with whom he felt a loathful brotherhood by the sympathy of all that was wicked in his heart. He could have well-nigh sworn that the shape of his own dead father beckoned him to advance, looking downward from a smoke wreath, while a woman, with dim features of despair, threw out her hand to warn him back. Was it his mother? But he had no power to retreat one step, nor to resist, even in thought, when the minister and good old Deacon Gookin seized his arms and led him to the blazing rock. Thither came also the slender form of a veiled female, led between Goody Cloyse, that pious teacher of the catechism, and Martha Carrier, who had received the devil's promise to be queen of hell. A rampant hag was she. And stood the proselytes beneath the canopy of fire.

"Welcome, my children," said the dark figure, "to the communion of your race. Ye have found thus young your nature and your destiny. My children, look behind you!"

They turned; and flashing forth, as it were, in a sheet of flame, the fiend worshipers were seen; the smile of welcome gleamed darkly on every visage.

"There," resumed the sable form, "are all whom ye have reverenced from youth. Ye deemed them holier than yourselves and shrank from your own sin, contrasting it with their lives of righteousness and prayerful aspirations heavenward. Yet here are they all in my worshiping assembly. This night it shall be granted you to know their secret deeds: how hoary-bearded elders of the church have whispered wanton words to the young maids of their households; how many a woman, eager for widows' weeds, has given her husband a drink at bedtime and let him sleep his last sleep in her bosom; how beardless youths have made haste to inherit their fathers' wealth; and how fair damsels —blush not, sweet ones—have dug little graves in the garden, and bidden me, the sole guest, to an infant's funeral. By the sympathy of your human hearts for sin ye shall scent out all the places—whether in church, bedchamber, street, field, or forest—where crime has been committed, and shall exult to behold the whole earth one stain of guilt, one mighty blood spot. Far more than this. It shall be yours to penetrate, in every bosom, the deep mystery of sin, the fountain of all wicked arts, and which inexhaustibly supplies more evil impulses than human power—than my power at its utmost—can make manifest in deeds. And now, my children, look upon each other."

They did so; and, by the blaze of the hell-kindled torches, the wretched man beheld his Faith, and the wife her husband, trembling before that unhallowed altar.

"Lo, there ye stand, my children," said the figure, in a deep and solemn tone, almost sad with its despairing awfulness, as if his once angelic nature could yet mourn for our miserable race. "Depending upon one another's hearts, ye had still hoped that virtue were not all a dream. Now are ye undeceived. Evil is the nature of mankind. Evil must be your only happiness. Welcome again, my children, to the communion of your race."

"Welcome," repeated the fiend worshipers, in one cry of despair and triumph.

And there they stood, the only pair, as it seemed, who were yet hesitating on the verge of wickedness in this dark world. A basin was hollowed, naturally, in the rock. Did it contain water, reddened by the lurid light? or was it blood? or, perchance, a liquid flame? Herein did the shape of evil dip his hand and prepare to lay the mark of baptism upon their foreheads, that they might be partakers of the mystery of sin, more conscious of the secret guilt of others, both in deed and thought, than they could now be of their own. The husband cast one look at his pale wife, and Faith at him. What polluted wretches would the next glance show them to each other, shuddering alike at what they disclosed and what they saw!

"Faith! Faith!" cried the husband, "look up to heaven, and resist the wicked one."

Whether Faith obeyed he knew not. Hardly had he spoken when he found himself amid calm night and solitude, listening to a roar of the wind which died heavily away through the forest. He staggered against the rock, and felt it chill and damp; while a hanging twig, that had been all on fire, besprinkled his cheek with the coldest dew.

The next morning young Goodman Brown came slowly into the street of Salem village, staring around him like a bewildered man. The good old minister was taking a walk along the graveyard to get an appetite for breakfast and meditate his sermon, and bestowed a blessing, as he passed, on Goodman Brown. He shrank from the venerable saint as if to avoid an anathema. Old Deacon Gookin was at domestic worship, and the holy words of prayer were heard through the open window. "What God doth the wizard pray to?" quoth Goodman Brown. Goody Cloyse, that excellent old Christian, stood in the early sunshine at her own lattice, catechizing a little girl who had brought her a pint of morning's milk. Goodman Brown snatched away the child as from the grasp of the fiend himself. Turning the corner by the meetinghouse, he spied the head of Faith, with the pink ribbons, gazing anxiously forth, and bursting into such joy at sight of him that she skipped along the street and almost kissed her husband before the whole village. But Goodman Brown looked sternly and sadly into her face, and passed on without a greeting.

Had Goodman Brown fallen asleep in the forest and only dreamed a wild dream of a witch meeting?

Be it so if you will; but alas! it was a dream of evil omen for young Goodman Brown. A stern, a sad, a darkly meditative, a distrustful, if not a desperate man did he become from the night of that fearful dream. On the Sabbath day, when the congregation were singing a holy psalm, he could not listen because an anthem of sin rushed loudly upon his ear and drowned all the blessed strain. When the minister spoke from the pulpit with power and fervid eloquence, and, with his hand on the open Bible, of the sacred truths of our religion, and of saint-like lives and triumphant deaths, and of future bliss or misery unutterable, then did Goodman Brown turn pale, dreading lest the roof should thunder down upon the gray blasphemer and his hearers. Often awaking suddenly at midnight, he shrank from the bosom of Faith; and at morning or eventide, when the family knelt down at prayer, he scowled and muttered to himself, and gazed sternly at his wife, and turned away. And when he had lived long, and was borne to his grave a hoary corpse, followed by Faith, an aged woman, and children and grandchildren, a goodly procession, besides neighbors not a few, they carved no hopeful verse upon his tombstone, for his dying hour was gloom.

Selected Bibliography

ALLSOP, KENNETH. "A Conversation with Arthur Miller," *Encounter,* July, 1959.

HOGAN, ROBERT. *Arthur Miller.* University of Minnesota Pamphlets, 1964.

MCCARTHY, MARY. "Naming Names: The Arthur Miller Case," *Encounter,* May, 1957.

POPKIN, HENRY. "Arthur Miller: The Strange Encounter," *Sewanee Review,* Winter, 1960.

SEAGER, ALLAN. "The Creative Agony of Arthur Miller," *Esquire,* October, 1959.

WELLAND, DENNIS. *Arthur Miller.* New York: Grove, 1961.

WILLIAMS, RAYMOND. "The Realism of Arthur Miller," *Critical Quarterly,* Summer, 1959.

NOTES

NOTES

NOTES

NOTES

NOTES

NOTES

NOTES